TOOLS FOR TEACHERS

- **ATOS:** 0.9
- **GRL:** D
- **WORD COUNT:** 59

- **CURRICULUM CONNECTIONS:** community helpers, firefighters

Skills to Teach

- **HIGH-FREQUENCY WORDS:** a, do, down, go, here, in, on, put, the, their, they, to
- **CONTENT WORDS:** alarm, bell, boots, coats, drill, firefighters, fire station, helmets, hoses, ladders, tools, truck
- **PUNCTUATION:** periods, exclamation marks, question mark, apostrophe
- **WORD STUDY:** long /i/, spelled i_e (fire, time), igh (fighters); /sh/, spelled ti (station); multisyllable words (alarm, firefighters, helmets, hoses, ladders, station)
- **TEXT TYPE:** factual description

Before Reading Activities

- Read the title and give a simple statement of the main idea.
- Have students "walk" though the book and talk about what they see in the pictures.
- Introduce new vocabulary by having students predict the first letter and locate the word in the text.
- Discuss any unfamiliar concepts that are in the text.

After Reading Activities

Explain to children that the fire firefighters in the story were practicing for a fire. Ask them what they think it means to practice something and why people might want to practice. Then encourage them to think about their own lives and whether there's anything they've ever needed to practice in order to get right. Discuss their answers as a group.

Tadpole Books are published by Jump!, 5357 Penn Avenue South, Minneapolis, MN 55419, www.jumplibrary.com

Copyright ©2018 Jump. International copyright reserved in all countries. No part of this book may be reproduced in any form without written permission from the publisher.

Editorial: Hundred Acre Words, LLC **Designer:** Anna Peterson

Photo Credits: 123RF: Bill Sinkovich, 2–3; Flashon Studio, 11; Tyler Olson, 8, 9, 10, 13. Alamy: FORGET Patrick/SAGAPHOTO.COM, 4–5; Susan Isakson, 12; tom carter, 14–15. Getty: PBNJ Productions, 7. iStock: Eriklam, 1; creisinger, 6. Shutterstock: Mega Pixel, cover; Digital Storm, cover; vilax, cover.

Library of Congress Cataloging-in-Publication Data
Names: Donner, Erica, author.
Title: Fire station / by Erica Donner.
Description: Minneapolis, Minnesota: Jump!, Inc., 2017. | Series: Around town | Includes index. | Audience: Ages 3–6.
Identifiers: LCCN 2017033888 (print) | LCCN 2017035161 (ebook) | ISBN 9781624967115 (ebook) | ISBN 9781620319253 (hardcover: alk. paper) | ISBN 9781620319260 (pbk.)
Subjects: LCSH: Fire stations—Juvenile literature. | Fire fighters—Juvenile literature.
Classification: LCC TH9148 (ebook) | LCC TH9148 .D63 2017 (print) | DDC 363.37—dc23
LC record available at https://lccn.loc.gov/2017033888

FIRE STATION

by Erica Donner

TABLE OF CONTENTS

tadpole
books

FIRE STATION

STATION 26

Let's go to the fire station.

Who works here?
Firefighters.

3

They do a drill.

Let's watch!

The alarm bell rings.

They go down the pole.

They put on coats.

boots

They put on boots.

helmet ···▶

They get their helmets.

tool

They get
their tools.

ladder

They check the ladders.

hose

They check the hoses.

They hop in the truck.

Time to go!

WORDS TO KNOW

boots

coat

helmet

hose

ladder

tool

INDEX

01/23 (3)